Ten seeds,

one ant.

Nine seeds,

one pigeon.

Eight seeds,

one mouse.

Seven shoots,

one slug.

Six shoots,

one mole.

Five seedlings,

one cat.

Four small plants,

one ball.

Three big plants,

one puppy.

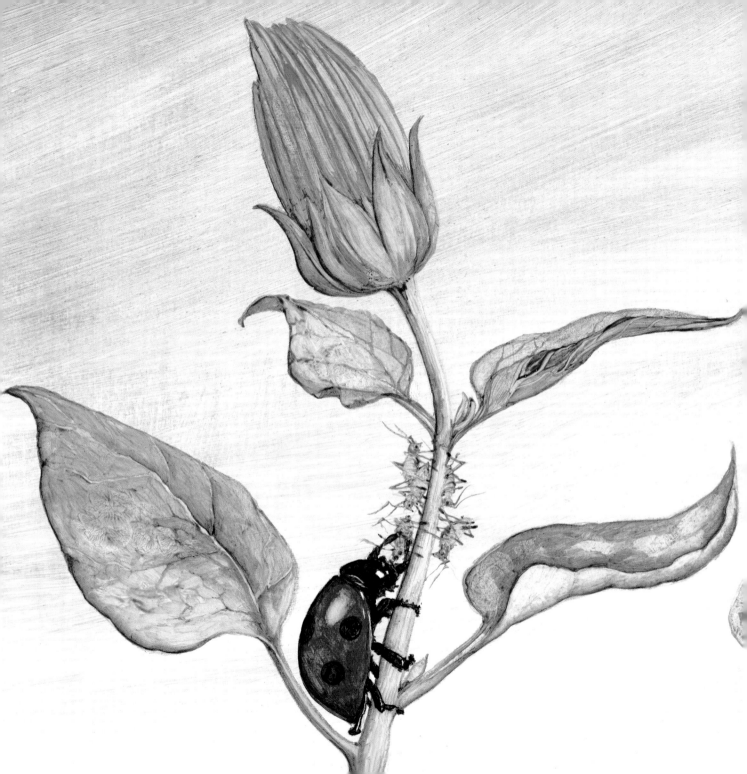

Two buds,

too many greenfly.

One flower,

one bee . . .

Ten Seeds!